Forest Resources of Mukundpur Satna Madhya Pradesh India

Chapter -1

<u>INTRODUCTION</u>

India, a land of physical, cultural, social and linguistic diversity is endowed by nature with enormous biological diversity. As a result India ranks amongst one of the 12 mega biodiversity countries of the world and harbors 17,000 flowering plant species. It accounts for 8% of the global biodiversity with only 2.4% of the total land area & the world (**Hajara and Mudgal 1997 and Reddy 2008**).

According to the International Union of Conservation of Nature (IUCN), it is estimated that the current species extinction rate is between 1000 and 10,000 times higher than it would naturally be. It is acknowledged that the future survival of humanity depends on the conservation and protection of natural wealth, and destruction of a species or a genetic line symbolizes the loss of a unique resource. This type of genetic and environmental impoverishment is irreversible. Changes in the structure in the multiplicity of resources lessen the society's scope to respond to new problems and opportunities, and there is the danger of new plant diseases or pests, climatic change due to the greenhouse effect and other setbacks. To overcome these hurdles, there is a need of coordinated efforts of scientists, government departments and nongovernmental organizations to undertake effective measure for conservation of plants.

A complete picture of threatened status, vulnerability and microclimate are yet has been determined. Conservation status is not properly documented till now. The present work has been taken to assess all relevant information on this aspect. An Assessment of threatened plants of India has been made by **Jain and Rao (1983)**. Biodiversity Threat assessment of Vindhyan region of Madhya Pradesh has been made by **Myres (1988); Nayar and Sastry (1987, 1988 & 1990); Nautiyal, et.al.(2003)**.

Conservation of Threatened species is important for maintaining the ecological balance of the habitat. Conservation of rate and endangered species of India as well as in different parts of world have been popularized through the propagation and preservation of these plant species in the botanical gardens or in the natural habitat. Conservation and economic evaluation of Biodiversity has been done by **Nayar, et.al. (1997).** Status and conservation of rare and endangered medicinal plant in the Indian Trans-Himalaya have been made by **Bush (1996); Kala (2000); Ayyad, et.al. (2000), Okigbo & Ogbogu (2008), Soetan & Aiyelaagbe et.al, (2009), Dubey et.al (2010), Oladele et.al. (2011).**

In addition to conservation objectives, the protected areas also have significant scientific, educational, cultural, recreational and spiritual values. These methods not only important to protect representative uniqueness of ecosystem and their rich biodiversity of different biogeography regions by regulating human and other biotic activities, but also ensure natural growth, proliferation and preparation of species as part of their natural ecosystem. One of the prime objectives of these protected areas is to assess and monitor diversity and dominance pattern at regular intervals, so that conservation status could be evaluated and maintained.

The studies on threatened medicinal plants of Andhra Pradesh and forest type have been made by **Reddy et.al. (2001) and Reddy (2007).** National special biodiversity assessment and the use of forest inventory data for a national protected area strategy in Guyana have been made by **Tersteege (1998) and Turpie (2004).** In Madhya Pradesh the forest are of various types and they provide diversity of vegetation. The varied nature of forests needs a thorough investigation of the soil, climate, bio-geochemical nature and Characteristics of vegetation.The central Indian state of Madhya Pradesh is one of the richest repositories of biological diversity. The state has diversity of ecosystems including plateaus, ravines, ridges, valleys, riparian areas and flat plains.

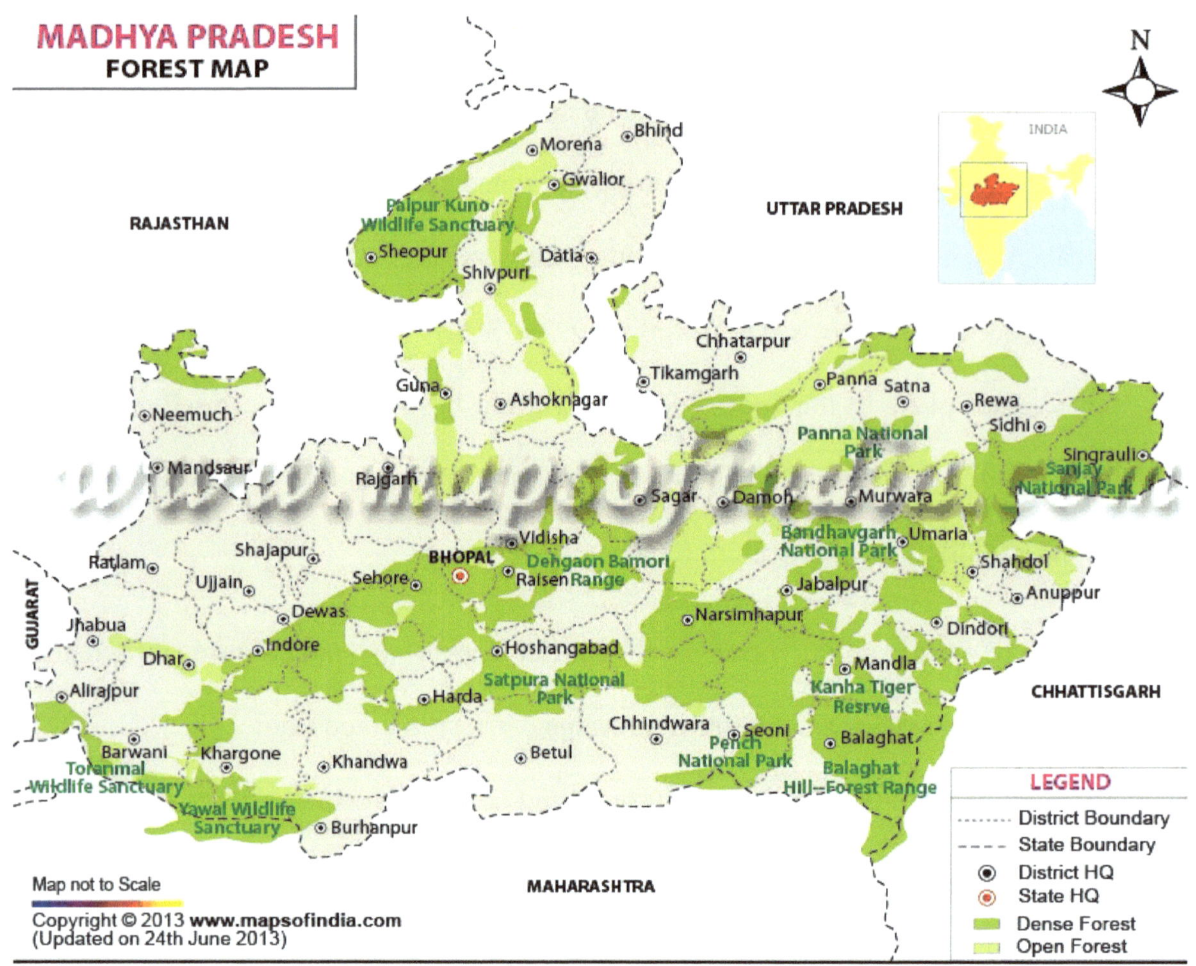

With four majors forest types, 10 national parks and 25 wildlife sanctuaries, the tiger state houses one of the richest faunal and floral diversity, with about 5000 plant species, these forests are habitat to as many as 500 birds species and 180 fish species.

Thousands of rice cultivars, a rich diversity of minor millets, indigenous cattle and poultry race like **Kadaknath** boasts of agro biodiversity. Home to six tribes with distinct customs, practices and diverse cultures, the biological diversity sustains livelihoods and ensures food security to two fifth of state population. Indigenous health systems nurtured by rich traditional knowledge woven about over 1000 medicinal plants contributed significantly to health security in rural areas.

In Satna district of the Madhya Pradesh, observation of Medicinal Importance of Sacred Plants of Chitrakoot Region Satna (M.P.) **Lipika Devi Bala and Ravindra Singh (2015)**. This paper discussed the 13 sacred plants species which are medicinally used by the tribes of Chirtakoot region district Satna Madhya Pradesh. The local people believe in the efficacy of these herbs along with some divine power, but the knowledge is restricted to very few elderly folks only.

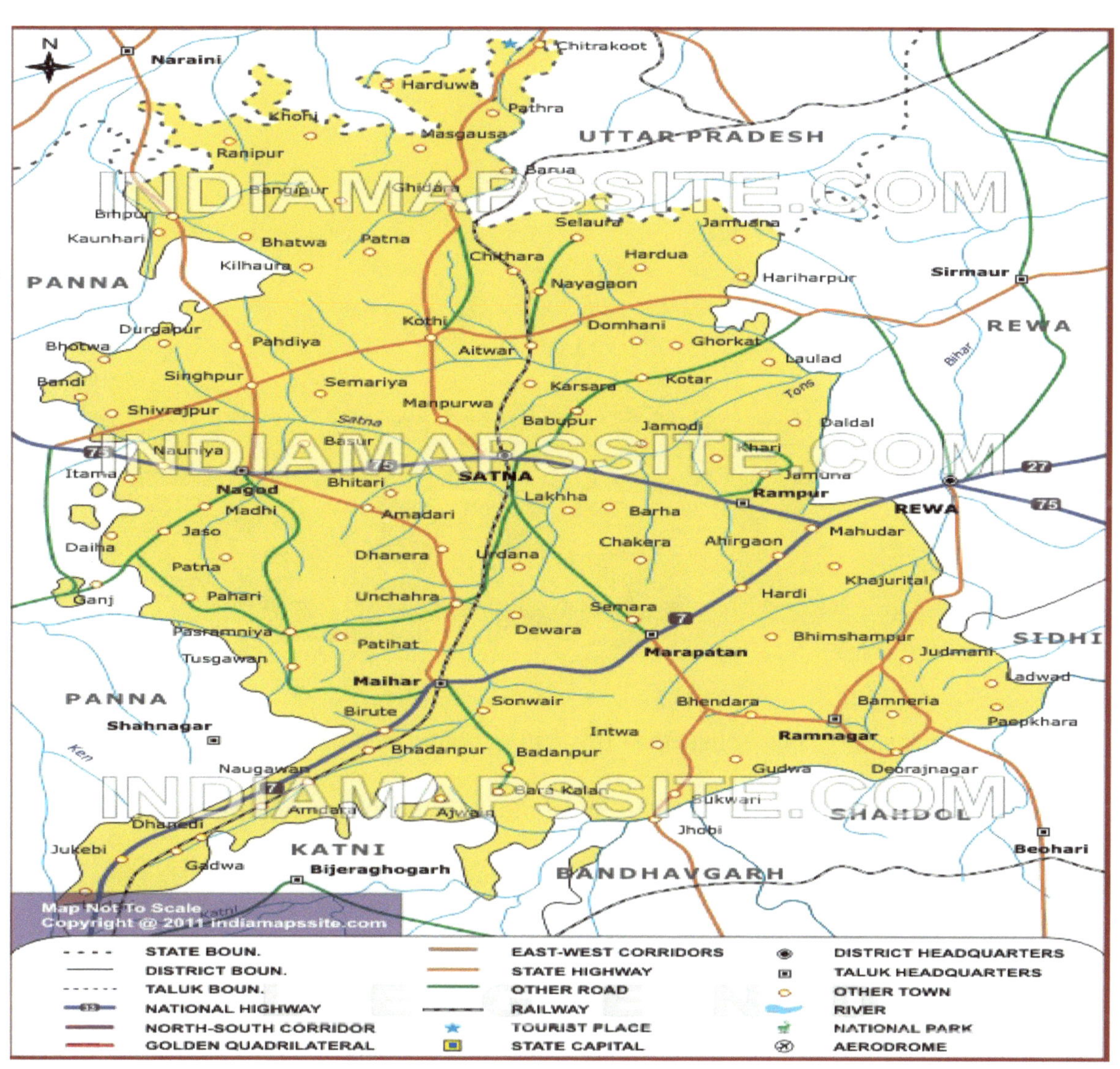

Therefore, this valuable information needs to be systematically collected, documented and preserved so that it can serve the mankind in generation to come and will also act as an important tool in conserving and preserving the traditional usage of these precious plant resources of high economic value. The collected information has been documented and presented in the current study.

The headquarters of Mukundpur range is in Mukundpur village, situated in Amarpatan Tahsil of Satna district in the state of Madhya Pradesh, India. It is the birth place of Mughal King Akbar II, 16th Mughal King.

The first white tiger safari is established at this village. The one of the mandate of this zoo and safari is to establish a small research centre for identification and propogation of various species of medicinal plants naturally occurring in adjoining forest areas.

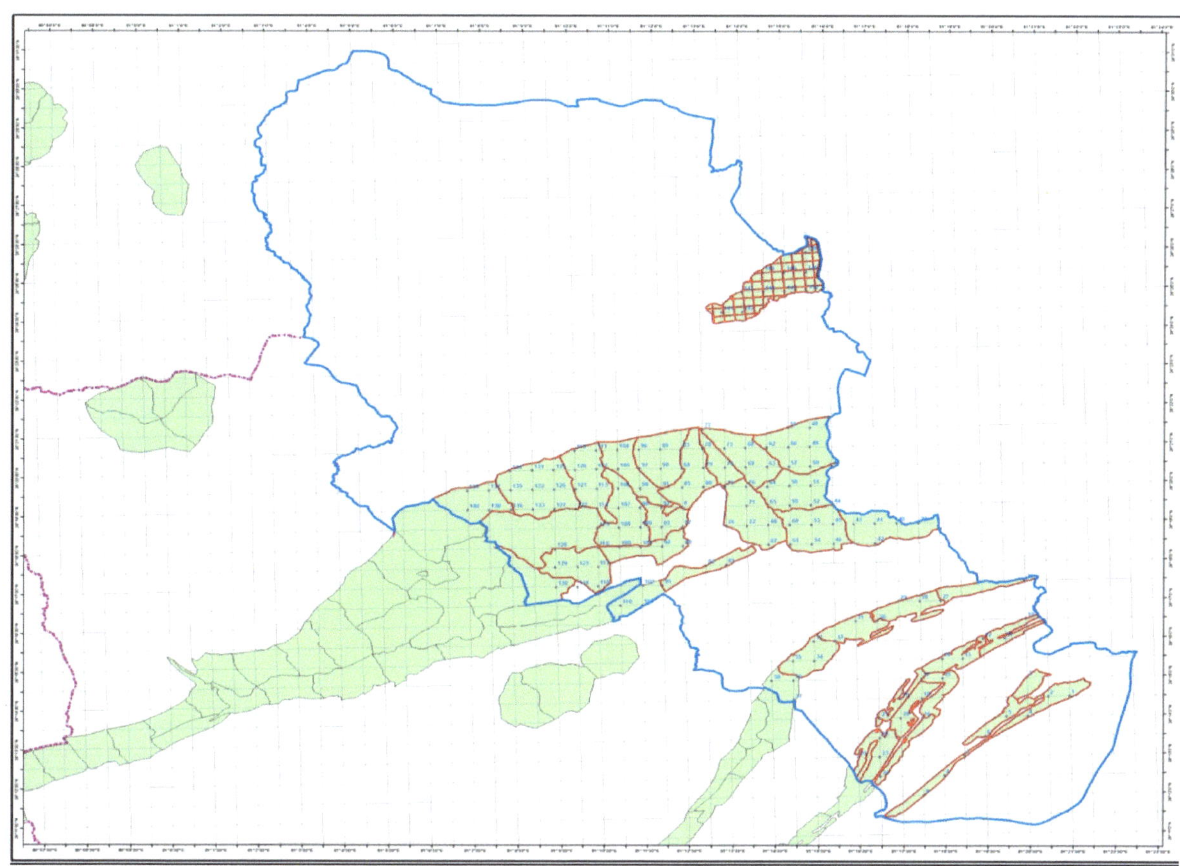

The Mukundpur range is surrounded by mining areas of bauxite (near Tikar village), limestone (Baghwar village) and other adjoining areas of Maihar and Bela. The adjoining cement factories are always in search of new areas and besides already exploiting old areas. The major industrial houses are applying for prospecting license (PL) for bauxite, iron, limestone etc. Though, it is essential for economic growth of the Vindhyan region.

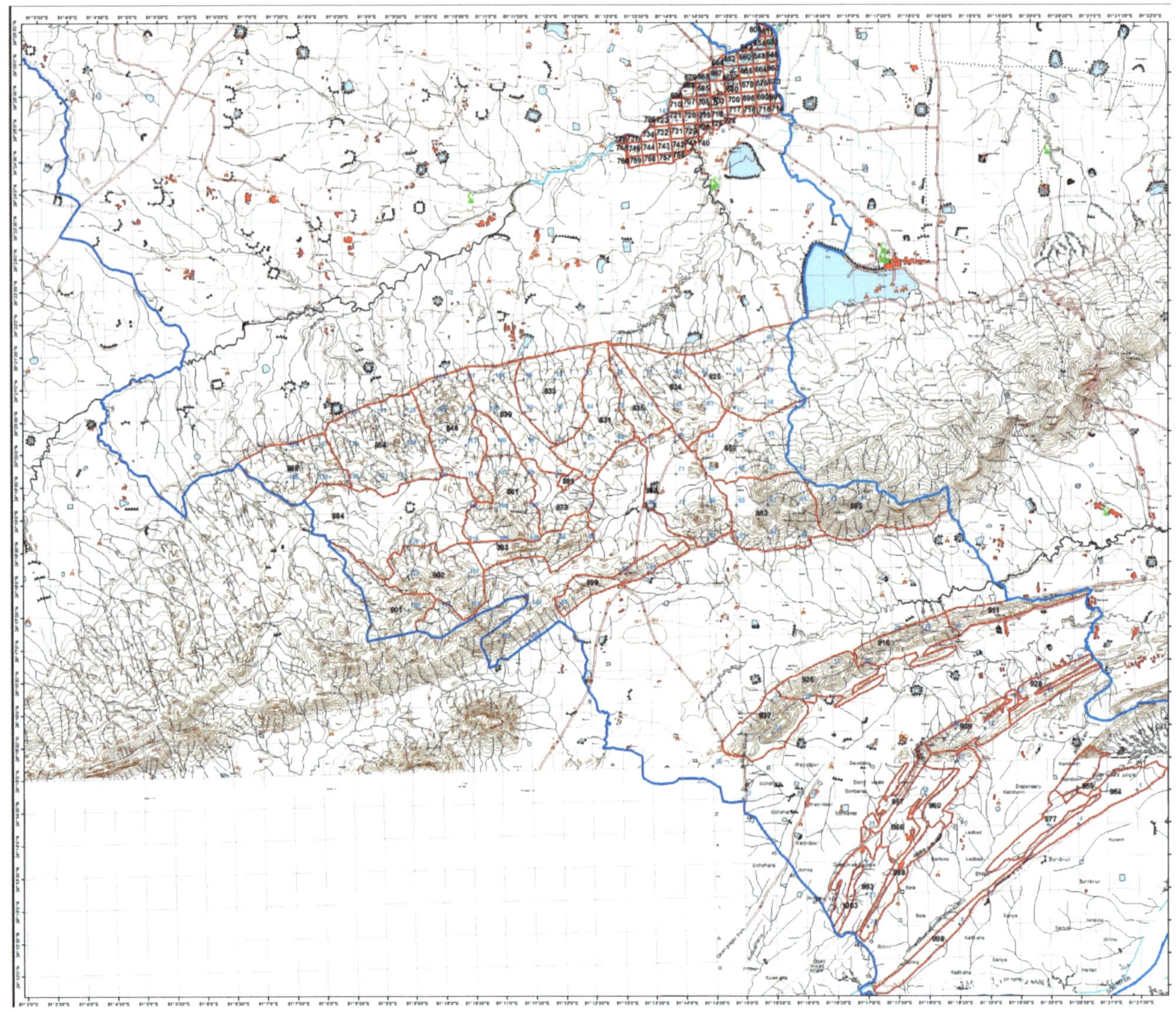

The forest area of Mukundpur range may be under high ecological stress in near future. These industrial houses may obtain non forest land as compensatory forest land in other district of Madhya Pradesh for diversion. But area of Mukundpur region will remain under high ecological stress zone.

Cement manufacturing is major cause for environmental pollution because lots of carbon dioxide is generated in the process. Carbon dioxide is a by-product. A chemical conversion process is used in the production of clinker a component of cement in which limestone ($CaCO_3$) is converted into lime (CaO). The CO_2 is emitted during cement production by fossil fuel combustion and is accounted for elsewhere. Cement industry across the world accounts for the

5% of global carbon dioxide emission due to intensive and extensive mining activities. Infrastructure development is also rapidly taking place in the area. Extensive road work ramification opens the area for plundering the certain species like *Gymnema sylvestre* (Gudmar) and *Tinospora cardifolia* (Giloy) and their commercial exploitation has posed the threat therefore it becomes of paramount importance that specific areas need to be studied floristically and enumeration and microclimatic conditions like soil be studied in depth which will go in long way for suitable management interventions and policy level changes. Mukundpur area has been historically famous and ecologically has come into limelight with initiation of white tiger safari therefore study in questions will go in long way to contribute suitably to knowledge.

Similarly the widening of various roads will cause heavy vehicular pollution in the area and also the fragmentation of habitat. For this future high ecological stress the study is very much important. Thus area is under high impact of temperature rise, industrialization, desertification and shift in the growing seasons of plants, loss of pollinators, seed dispersers and increasing frequency of intense weather events such as drought storms and floods making several valuable plants extinct **(Bapat et al 2008, Gardener et al 2009).** This year of 2016 has witnessed the same flood situation in the area.

Thus with this backdrop role of botanist assumes the prime significance to undertake the critical study of plant bio-diversity and its management along with the evaluation of soil parameters in *Mukundpur* region of *Satna* district of Madhya Pradesh, India. The studies of following objectives are to taken as:-

    i)   Identification and characterization of an endangered plant and their study of taxonomy, ecology and physiology.

    ii)   To understand the reasons for a particular plant becoming endangered.

iii)   Propagation of the plant under controlled environment followed by in situ and ex situ conservation.

iv)   To create a self-sustainable population of threatened species in their natural habitat and compilation of database and documentation of all threatened plants.

v)   To explore the utility of an endangered plant, if any, for basic as well as commercial applicability.

vi)   To study the soil parameters should be linked with threatening status and plant diversity for future mining strategy of the area.

Thus detailed study is needed for the biodiversity conservation to maintain the current level as well as to stop any further decline.

With the above objectives for present study following concept and thought has been presented.

Resource is a commodity for benefit of the mankind. Forest resources of the study area have timber product and non timber product used by local people and commercial purposes. In Madhya Pradesh the forest management is done by forest department through working plans. Hence assessment of forest resource is integral component of the management. Forest resources is treated as a crop hence silviculture restoration and conservation is done. For the maintenance and enhancement of forest health and viltalty the status of regeneration is also done as a management. Hence forest resources survey is done by assessing the species by number of trees and its volume and regeneration. The other species of vegetations like shrubs, herbs, lianas (woody climbers) are also assessed. On the basis of this assessment past performance is evaluated and future management is prescribed. The status of species prone to over exploitation is also done in the management by using the principle of sustainable harvest. In this principle the annual increment of the forest crop is only harvested.

Forest is also a terrestrial eco system which has living and non living component. The flora and fauna are the living components and soil and rocks are non living component. The energy transfer and nutrient cycling are the two functions in eco system. Energy transfer take place in living component in which the solar energy is converted into chemical energy. The various species of vegetation in forests have various traping efficiency of the solar energy, which create different compostion of vegetation in forests in the presence, number and dominance under particular climate, rock and soil. Thus ecological study is done by evaluating IVI (Important Value Index). The threat and conservation category assessment is also done in this study because the forest management practices overlook the ecological aspects.

The nutrient cycling takes place from non living components to living components and living components to non living components. Since rock, soil in the forest is the store house of the nutrient the various soil parameters will play important role in ecological function of the forest. Hence in the present study the soil parameters like pH, electrical conductivity, availability of major nutrients (Nitirogen, Phosphorous and Potassium) and micro nutrients like (Copper, Manganisum, Iron and Zink) are studied with various species of Important value Index and in various forest types density, age and site quality classes. This will help in restoration of species in the management of the forest.

After analyzing the threatening status of various species of vegetation, species which require protection, there phenological study is made so that there flowering, fruiting status can be monitored for future management. Again the ethnobotanincal use and there plant part analysis study is also recorded for proper use of those threatened species of vegetation for future management. The conservation and management strategies are also discussed in the study.

Chapter -2

Ecology and Climatic Condition of Mukundpur range

2.1 Site Characteristics-

Mukundpur region mainly comprises the present area of Mukundpur range of Satna forest division. The range has geographical area of 589.71 km^2 with forest area 111.55 km^2. The area lies between north latitude of 24^0 11'35" to 24^0 26'25" and east longitude of 81^0 6'35" to 81^0 22'20". The famous world white tiger safari is also situated in northern side of this range.

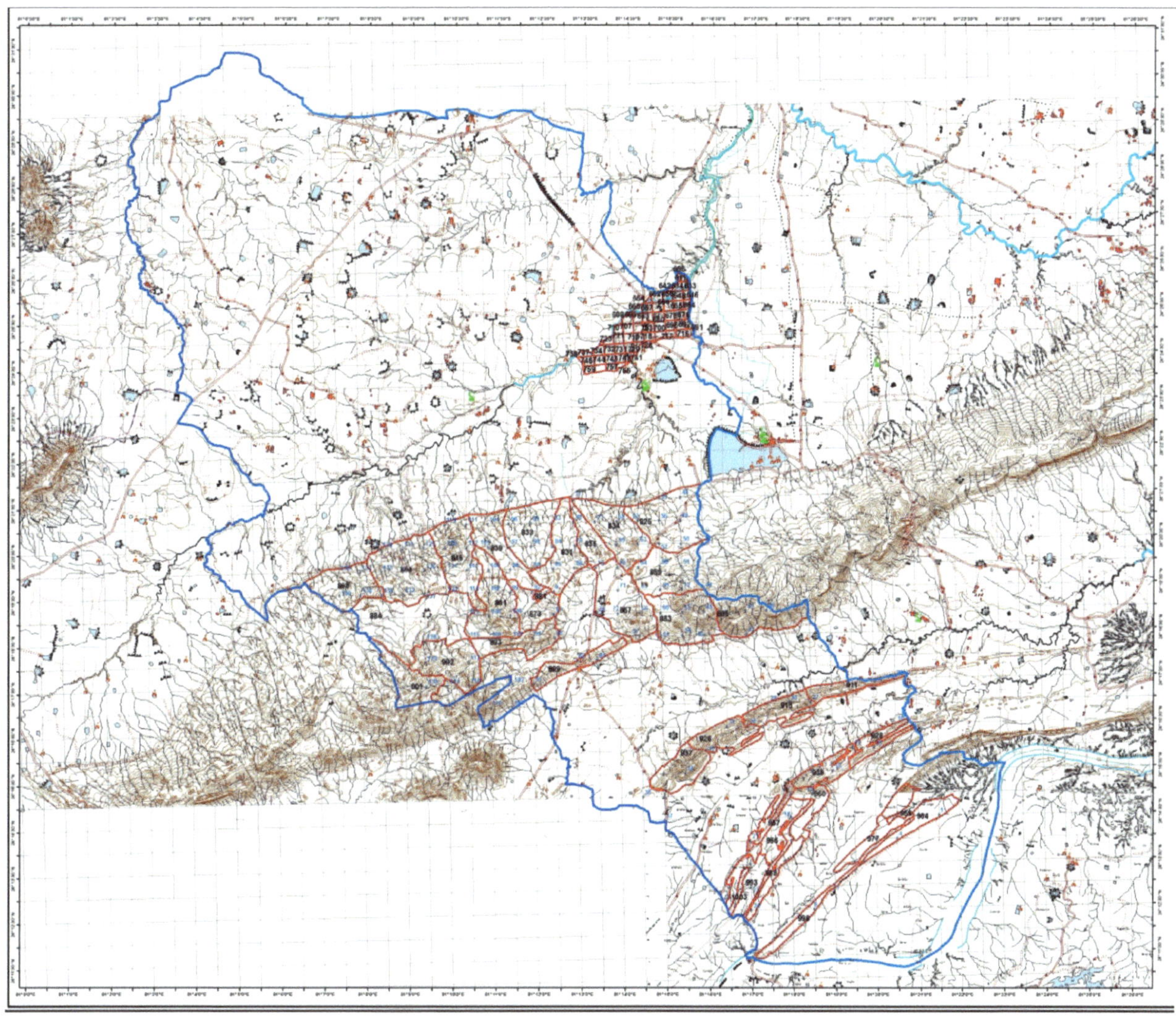

The forest area of this range exists in 7 forest blocks namely Mand, Govindgarh extension, Papra, Jhinna, Sarhai, Kokahansar and Mankesar. The forest blocks of Govindgarh extension and papra extend in Satna and Rewa forest districts. The part of Mankesar forest block lies in submerged area of Bansagar dam.

Boundary details of the area

Northern boundary lies with Beehar River demarcating Satna and Rewa district. The forest of Mand reserve it's situated in this area where first white tiger safari is established.

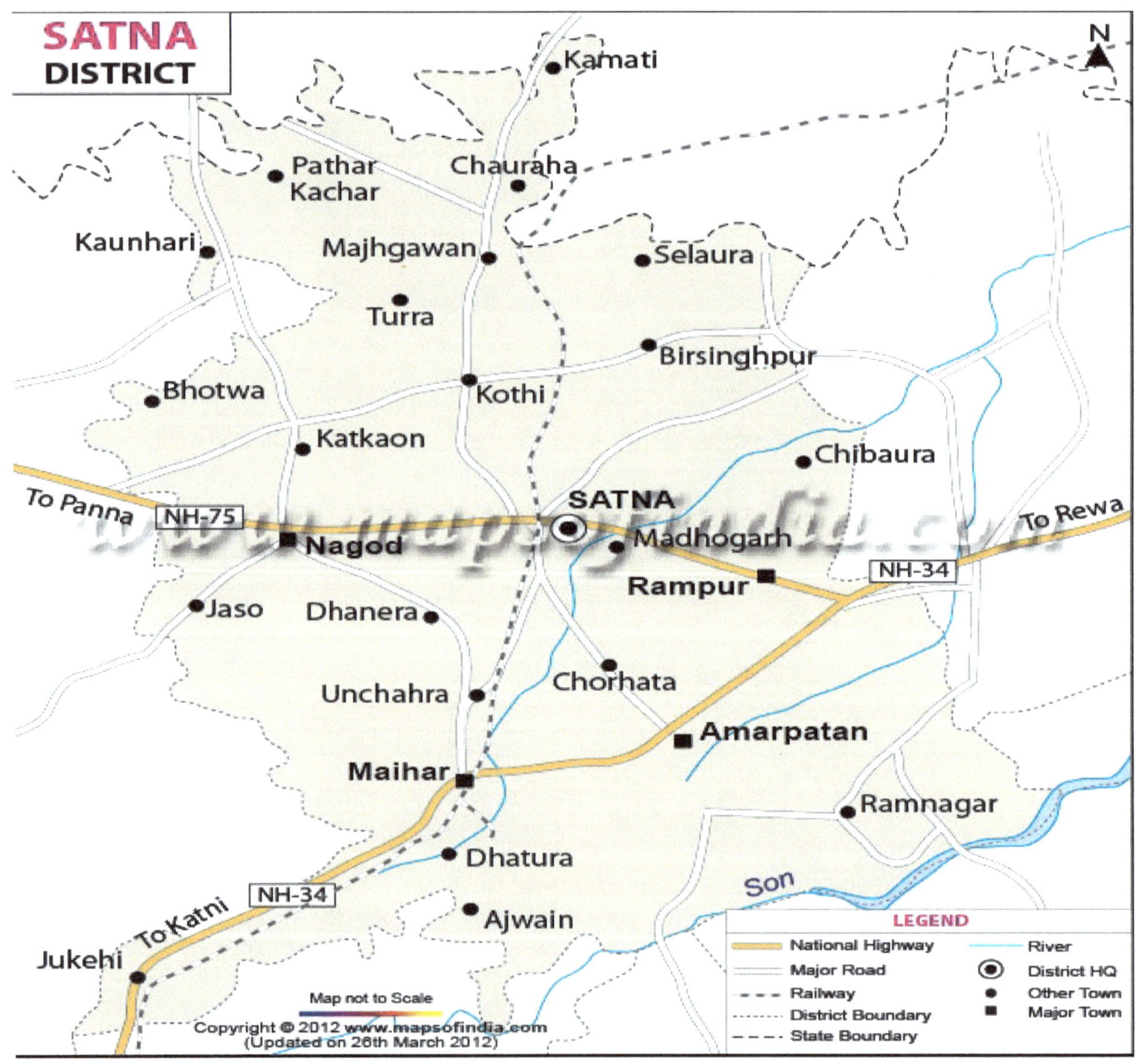

Eastern boundary lies mainly with the district boundaries bifurcating Rewa and Satna districts. The famous Charaki ghati forms one of its boundaries. Southern boundary lies mainly with submerged area of Son River and it extends to district boundaries of Shahadol and Satna districts. The western boundaries of the study area spread along the forest boundary of Amarpatan range.

Topography of the area

The land masses of the study area are extended normally in alternate series of plains and hilly region. The agricultural practices are extended in plains while forests are mainly in hilly region. The earth surface of study area may be classified as:

1) Satna and Rewa Plateau

2) Kaimur mountain ranges

3) Northern Vindhyan mountains

Satna and Rewa Plateau

The surface of this Plateau exists between Vindhyan and Kaimur Mountains. The study area of this plateau is in mainly plains. The Beehar River is in the north western boundary while Papra pahad forms south eastern boundary.

Kaimur mountain ranges

This mountain ranges bifurcate the Satna and Rewa plateau with Son valley. It extends from south western to north eastern direction. These mountain range acts as natural barrier between south and north. The slopes of these ranges have the special features as northern slopes are low while southern slopes are very steeps and even vertical at some places.

Northern Vindhyan Mountains

Northern Vindhyan Mountains form the part of Satna Rewa plateau. The slopes of these ranges are in northern directions.

2.2 Edaphic factors of Mukundpur range-

The soil in the study area has the origin of Vindhyan formation and it consists of materials from sand stone, limestone and shale. The soil is mainly siliceous, aluminous and stony nature. It is lateritic in some places. The physical and chemical characteristics of the soil mainly depend on parent rock material. These are also affected by physical factors, climate and vegetation. Thus the types of soil depend mainly on time, parent rock material, slopes and vegetations. The soil has poor water holding capacity. The forests of study area have poor availability of nitrogen and potassium though availability of phosphorus is high. The availability of zinc and manganese is also poor but iron and copper elements are sufficient in study area.

The soil is a very complex medium. The soil contains mineral matter, organic matter, water and air. Mineral matter in the soil occurs in the form of mineral particles. The soil textures of study area have various combination of mineral particles varing from coarse textured soil to light soil. In some areas the gravels are also noticed. The soil structure is granular to fine and at some places it is compacted due to heavy grazing and fire. In Mand forest reserve the soil is black cotton but it is stony, gravely in other areas of Mukundpur range. The soil has a normal pH, electrical conductivity, medium organic matter and phosphorus containt, while low availbilty of nitrogen and potassium. The soil of study area has sufficient copper and Iron while it is deficient in Zince and manganese. The humus containt is insufficient at high mountain ridges and it is sufficient in other areas. The status of erosion is higher in hills but other areas it is less. The gully formations are more near Nallas and Rivers.

2.3 Geology and phyto geography of region-

2.3.1 General geology of the area

Geologically, the area is part of the Semri Group of the Vindhyan Super group. The rock consists of calcareous and argillaceous sediments which occupy almost the entire area. The limestone is well bedded, horizontal and highly jointed with occasional folding. The shale, limestone and glauconitic beds are lying above the silicified and porcellanite rocks together from the Khenjua stage. They show ripple marks, finely laminated and other sedimentary characters pointing to shallow water deposition. Exposures of these formations are met with in central and southern parts of the study area as seen in and around Ramnagar, Hinauti, Baghwar, Saguni, Jigna, Gorsari. The topmost horizon of the semri series made up of alternate, thinly bedded, layers of shale and Rohtash limestone. They are grey and pink in color. The grayish varieties are usually thickly bedded massive and lenticular in shape. The outcrops of this rock are well exposed in and around Biharganj, Mirgauti, Jurmani, Argat villages. In the study area Rohtas Limestone is mainly exposed in the South and South-East of Govindgarh area. Mostly the limestone is exposed in flat areas are forming low hillocks. The exposed thickness of Rohtas Limestone is about 55 meters. In general it is horizontally disposed with ENE-WSW strike and 5^0 to 10^0 northerly dips. It is generally light grey in color (occasionally dark) and thickly to thinly bed with occasionally development of minor contortions. Majority of the limestone appear to be fine grained with interbedded coarse grained type. Sedimentary structures like ripple marks of different types have been noticed but they are not widespread. Stylolitcs of low amplitudes are common in the area however flat pebble conglomeratic bands, burrow like structures and mud cracks are also observed. It is subdivided into four groups:

Upper Vindhyan-   Thickness (m)

                      Bhander Group   1000 m

                      Rewa Group   2000 m

                      Kaimur Group   400 m

Lower Vindhyan   Samri Group   1300 m

The Semri group is referred to as the Lower Vindhyan wherea Kaimnr, Rewa and Bhander group as the upper vindhyan.

2.3.2 Rock types of the study area

The rock types of Lower and Upper vindhyan supergroup have been den roped in the study are the brief description of each unit is as below:

Semri Group: The semri group is divisible unit: Basal, Porcellantits, Kheinjua and Rohtas stoge. The kheinjua formation which entrains shale and limestone is developed in the area. The limestone is developed into eastern port of the area. It is black to gray in color and represented by cherty limestone. It shows the development of stromatolile.

Kheinjua shale is black to reddish brown in color thinly bedded and finely laminated character. It is developed in the southern port of the area. At places polygonal mud eracks are well developed in the shale.

Rohtas limestone

It is light Grey to dark Greg in color. It is slightly reddish at few places due to iron. It is go fine to medium grained, hard, compact bedded and massive. It is dolomitised in nature. Its thickness is up to 50 meter. It is the main lithounits of the area. It is divisible in to three horizons.

i)   Thinly bedded to blocky limestone and dolomitic limestone.

ii)   Cherty nodular limestone

iii) Shaly limestone

The Rohtas limestone is interstratified with shale bands up to 2 meter thick. The shale is usually argillaceous but at its contact with the limestone it becomes calcareous and finally grades into lime one.

Limestone is the most important widespread rock types and extremely complex in their genesis and diagenesis. They are generally monocoystalline and texturally diverse and polygenetic. The petrographic characters of Rohtas limestone indicate grains are mainly intraclasts, oolites, pellets. In the Rohtas Limestone only intraclast is developed. The intraclast is defined as sand sized or slightly larger particles in limestones, texturally analogous to rock fragments (**Folk 1959**). These are reworked products of a weakly consolidated substrate with in basin of deposition. The intraclasts associated with Rohtas Limestone are light coloured, derived by the fragmentation of argillaceous limestone matrix. The framework grains occur either in micritic or sparry matrix. Micrite is part of the rock in which all the allochemical and terrigeneous sediment particles are embedded. Micrite is one of the essentially normal precipitates (including inorganic and biochemical) formed within the basin of deposition. Micrite is categorized as minimicrite, micrite and microsparite depending upon grain size. The limestone of the area are mainly micritic however they are showing signs of crystallization when fine grained and appears as faintly transluscent with a slightly brownish colour. In Rohtas Limestone it is difficult to envisage a single cause for the genesis of micrite. The possibility of biological activity in the Rohtas Limestone and also transported origin can not be suggested due to lack of secondary sedimentary structures. It seems that micrite of Rohtas limestone may be insitu origin (automicrite) of inorganic precipitation of aragonite mud due to change in salinity and temperature of water. Sparite is calcite grains of more than 10 microns in diameter (**Folk 1959**) and is distinguished from micrite by its clarity and transparency as well defined grain boundaries and cleavage traces. The grains are cement filling pre-existing cavities and pores and if these are large the grains can reach a size well over a millimeter. It occurs in granular, drusy and fibrous forms called orthosparite. Besides this type of sparite, there are large spars developed from micrite known as psudosparite. This change of micrite into coarsely crystalline calcite is called nemorphism which is well pronounced in the Rohtas Limestone. The most characteristic texture of Rohtas Limestone can be termed as crystalline texture of **Friedman and Sanders (1978).** The crystalline textures associated with Rohtas Limestones are of mostly diagenetic in origin and most of them are extensively modified or destroyed during diagenesis (**Bathurst, 1975**). Rohtas Limestone of the area has been subjected to various diagenetic processes. The diagenesis of carbonate rocks is very complex because of their unstable mineralogy and because of their high initial permeability, making them susceptible to percolating reacting fluids. Good summaries of diagenetic environments in carbonates have been published by **Folk (1974), Matthews (1975), Bathurst (1976), Friedman and Sanders (1978) and Longman (1980).**

Baghawar Shale: It is overlies on Rohtas limestones and light grey to greenish grey in colour. It contains one mica minerals. Some sedimentary stonetures like mud cracks, ripple marks are associated with this formation.

Kaimur Quartzite

It is also known as Dhandranl Quartxite and well developed in Jigna area. It is light pick, white and brown in colour and contains mainly (79%) silica mineral. It compreses thickly bedded, massive and lenticular sandstone nature.

Rewa Group

(Around govindgarh Area) It is represented by Jhirishale and govindgarh sandstone in the area. Jhirishale is chacolale brown in colour with thickness of about 3 meter. Vatious sedimentary strnctures are well developed in the study area.

Govindgarh sandstone light pink, steal grey white coarse grained to medium grained sandstone. It is thickly bedded, massive and cross bedded sandstone. Chemically it mature sandstone and contains mainly quartz and feldspar minerals. Ripple marks, convolute bedding is the common sedimentary structures.

Bhander Group (Mukundpur, Ramnagar, Amarpatan Area) the ganurgash, Bhander limestone, sirbu shale are the main lithounits of the Bhander group. It the study area ganurgarh shale and Bhander limestone are developed. The ganargarh shale is brown to reddish brow in colour it is about 4 meter in thickness with well developed lamination.

Bhander limestone is most important lithounit or the Bhander group. It is light to dark grey in colour. Its thickness varies from 10 meter to 15 meter. It is stromatolitic and non stromatolitic type in nature chemically it contains mainly calcile and silica mineral. One to high content of CaO, it is useful for cement. It is more or less horizontal types.

2.4 Climate of study area

This data is taken from meterological observatory of agriculture collage Rewa.

Table 2.1

Month	Rainfall (MM)		Temperature C^0				Relative Humidity (%)			
	2015	2016	2015		2016		2015		2016	
			Max	Min	Max	Min	Max	Min	Max	Min
January	12.9	39.8	19.13	8.8	19.7	7.7	76.16	70.35	75.6	69.4
February	19.6	19.4	24.8	10.15	23.7	9.1	75.6	45.57	75.06	44.7
March	00	00	31.5	13.64	33.2	14.64	70.45	48.38	70.71	48.3
April	27.8	16.2	36.66	18.33	36.1	19.3	68.76	31.03	70.6	32.3
May	20.3	38.6	43.8	21.4	42.1	20.6	70.23	33.07	70.1	32.1
June	119.8	65.6	40.3	20.5	43.7	21.1	69.23	38.06	67.23	30.2
July	169.14	183.7	34.2	18.9	34.2	19.9	76.2	41.20	75.1	40.8
August	156.6	196.4	32.7	16.6	31.7	15.6	81.13	42.7	78.1	41.7
September	185.7	205.1	29.2	15.7	28.2	14.6	83.3	43.1	80	41.7
October	93.8	137.4	27.3	13.1	26.2	13.3	70.85	38.7	83.3	45.1
November	10.3	48.5	24.3	11.4	23.3	11.2	74.24	40.3	73.15	37.1
December	21.6	19.6	20.9	9.7	19.9	9.5	74.68	40.5	73	39.4
	837.54	970.3								

Meteorological observation of study area of Mukundpur is nearest to this observatory. The rainfall, maximum and minimum temperature and relavive humidity in percentage is express in table for years 2015 and 2016 for different months from January to December.

Rainfall

The total annual rainfall recorded in the years 2015 and 2016 are 837.54 mm and 970.3 mm. Thus the mean annual rainfall for the two years are 904.92 mm.

The line diagram for the years of 2015 and 2016 for various months are shown in following graphs. From the graphs it is evident that the rainfall month are middle of June to middle of september. The dry months are January, Febuary, March, April, October, November and December.

The area receives the precipitation in the months of middle of June to Middlie of September. Though, it receives the winter precipitation also. The average rainy days are nearly 33 to 38 days in last years.

Figure 2.1

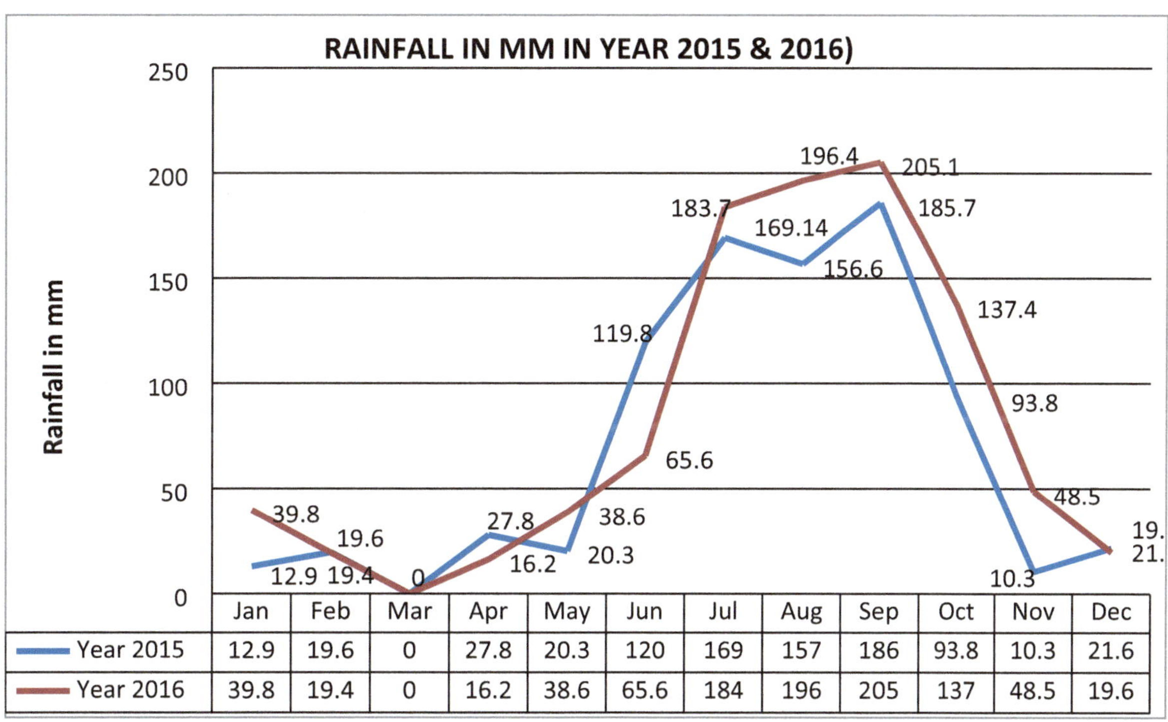

	Jan	Feb	Mar	Apr	May	Jun	Jul	Aug	Sep	Oct	Nov	Dec
Year 2015	12.9	19.6	0	27.8	20.3	120	169	157	186	93.8	10.3	21.6
Year 2016	39.8	19.4	0	16.2	38.6	65.6	184	196	205	137	48.5	19.6

This area has also witnessed the flood situation in this year of 2016. Though, the rainfall data do not suggest this. There may be reason that the rivers and nalas have received the heaviest rainfall in upper reaches and flood situation has been from in lower reaches of Mukundpur and Rewa region.

Temperature

The line diagram for maximum and minimum temperature for the years 2015 and 2016 for different months are depicted in the following graphs. From the graph it is clear that the hottest months are April to June, while coldest months are November, December, January, February and middle March. The moderate months are July, August, September and October. The lowest temperature recorded in the month of January with average minimum temperature 8.75 ^{0}C for the years 2015 and 2016.

Figure 2.2

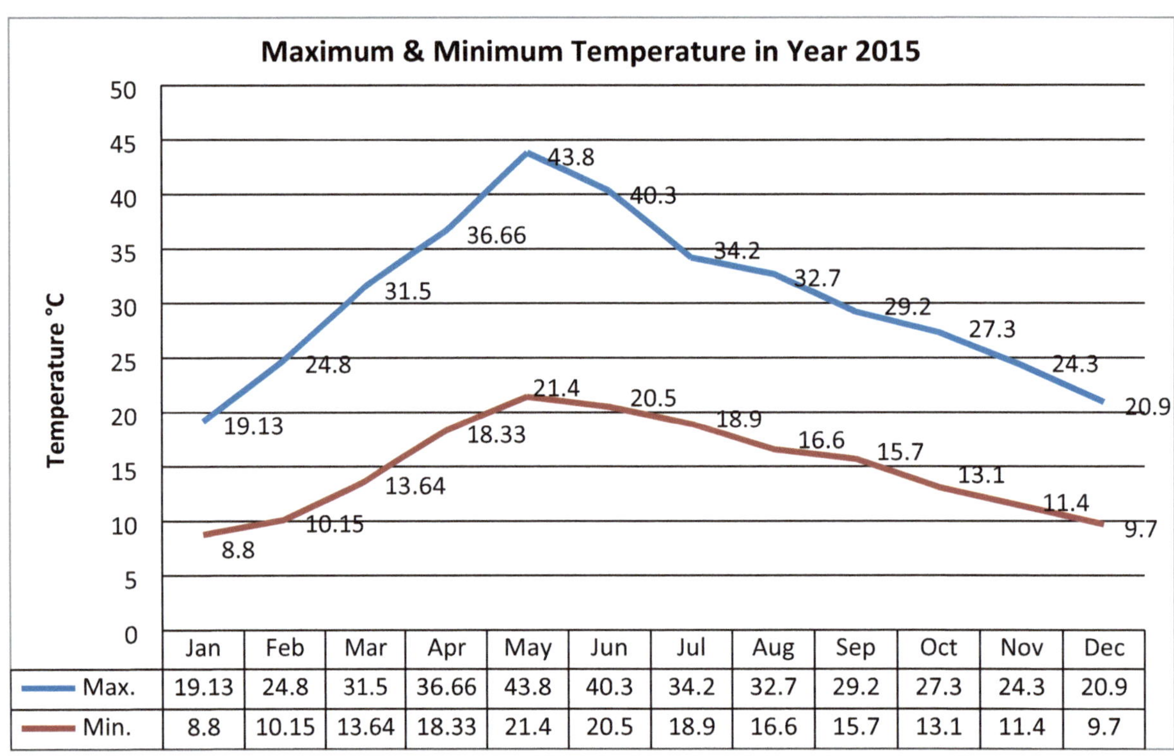

	Jan	Feb	Mar	Apr	May	Jun	Jul	Aug	Sep	Oct	Nov	Dec
Max.	19.13	24.8	31.5	36.66	43.8	40.3	34.2	32.7	29.2	27.3	24.3	20.9
Min.	8.8	10.15	13.64	18.33	21.4	20.5	18.9	16.6	15.7	13.1	11.4	9.7

Figure 2.3

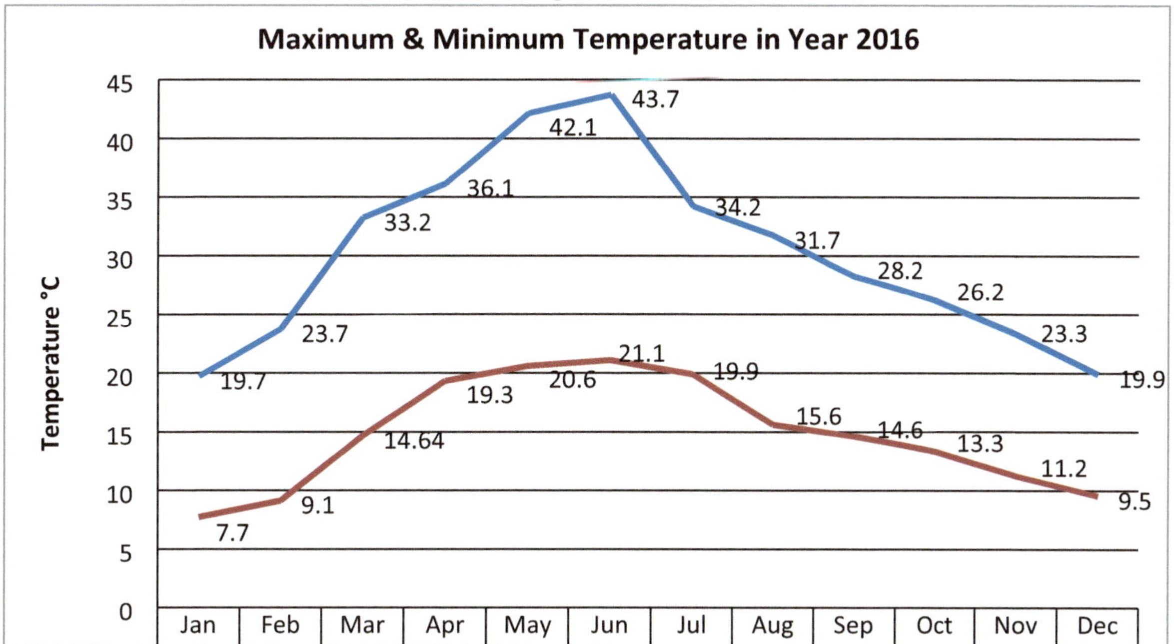

	Jan	Feb	Mar	Apr	May	Jun	Jul	Aug	Sep	Oct	Nov	Dec
Max.	19.7	23.7	33.2	36.1	42.1	43.7	34.2	31.7	28.2	26.2	23.3	19.9
Min.	7.7	9.1	14.64	19.3	20.6	21.1	19.9	15.6	14.6	13.3	11.2	9.5

The maximum temperature recorded in the month of May with average maximum temperature of 42.95⁰C.

Relative Humidity

The line diagram for maximum and minimum relative humidity for the years 2015 and 2016 for different months are depicted in the following graphs. The relative humidity is the maximum in the months of September though the humid months are July, August, September. The lowest humidity is in the months of April, May and June. The average maximum relative humididty is 81.6% that exists in the months of September and average minimum humidity is 31.17 % which exists in the months of April. The maximum relative humidity ranges between 69.43 to 81.65 % while minimum relative humidity ranges between 30.75 to 69.9 %.

Figure 2.4

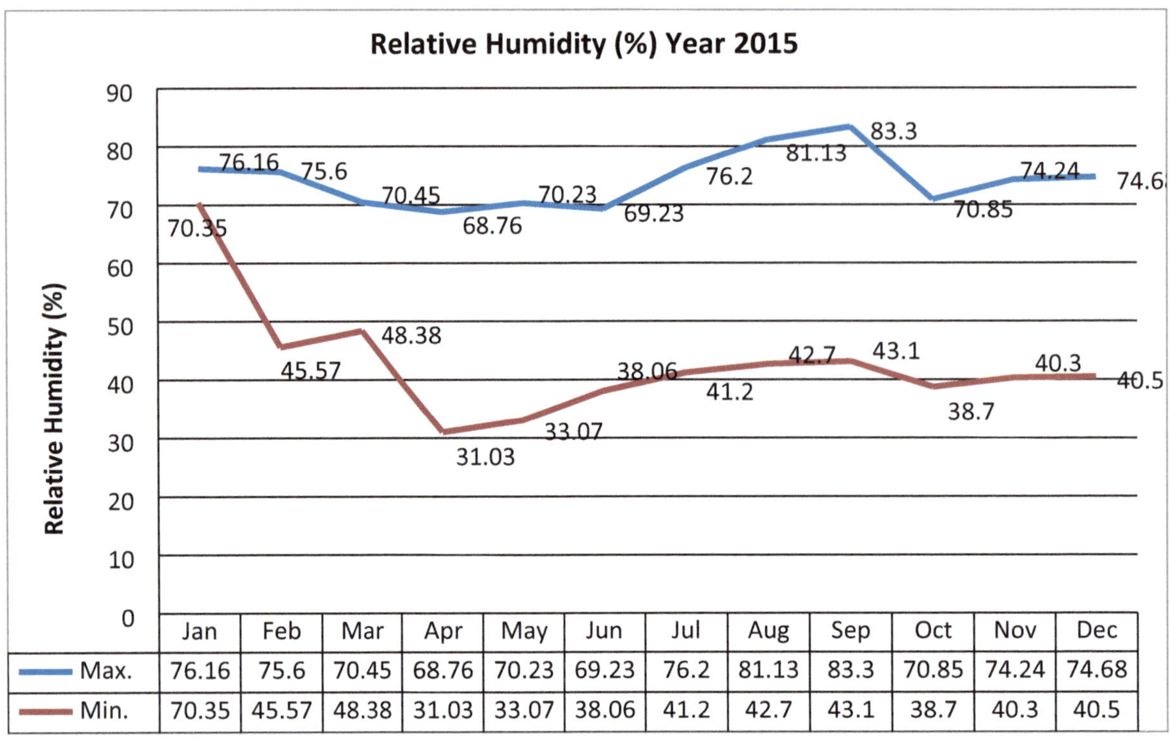

	Jan	Feb	Mar	Apr	May	Jun	Jul	Aug	Sep	Oct	Nov	Dec
Max.	76.16	75.6	70.45	68.76	70.23	69.23	76.2	81.13	83.3	70.85	74.24	74.68
Min.	70.35	45.57	48.38	31.03	33.07	38.06	41.2	42.7	43.1	38.7	40.3	40.5

Figure 2.5

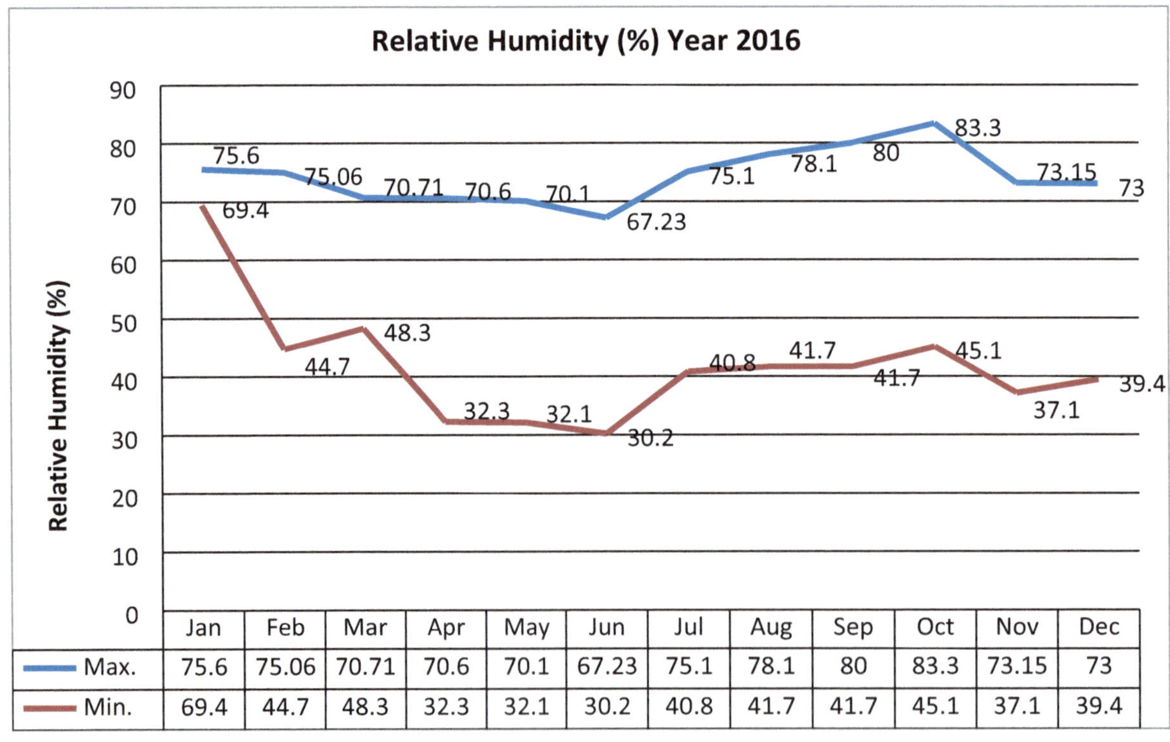

	Jan	Feb	Mar	Apr	May	Jun	Jul	Aug	Sep	Oct	Nov	Dec
Max.	75.6	75.06	70.71	70.6	70.1	67.23	75.1	78.1	80	83.3	73.15	73
Min.	69.4	44.7	48.3	32.3	32.1	30.2	40.8	41.7	41.7	45.1	37.1	39.4

The graph shows that minimum lowest humidity 69.9 % which may be due to the fog that exists in the months of January.

2.5 Vegetation Characteristics of the study area

The Mukundpur range has eight forest blocks with total forest area 111.55 km^2. The characterstics of vegetation and type of forests mainly depend on climate, geology, parent rock materials and types of soil. The diversity and compositions of forests mainly depend on rainfall, temperature, altitude, aspects and slopes. The major the study areas has northern tropical dry deciduous mixed forest with some patches of southern tropical dry deciduous teak forests specially in Mand reserve. The results of stock mapping done by working plan of satna have been used for analysis of forest resource survey as a secoundary data.

From the results of stock mapping done by working plan officer Satna the following table shows the forest type and density classification as below:

Table 2.2

S. No.	Forest type	Density of forest type					Total area (ha)
		Stocked (ha)	under Stocked (ha)	Blank (ha)	Encroac hment (ha)	Rivers, Nala, Ponds, mines etc (ha)	
1	Sal	7.796	117.56				125.356
2	Teak	473.385	86.943				560.328
3	Mixed	23.947	4381.424				4405.371
Total Area in (ha.)		505.128	4585.927	5490.047	559.108	14.948	11155.158

From the above table it is clear that the area has mainly Sal, Sagon and mixed forest types.

The compositions of main vegetation are as follows:-

1. **Top canopy** - *Anogeissus latifolia, Diospyros melanoxylon, Terminalia tomentosa, Lannea coromandelica, Sterculia urens, Boswellia serrata, Madhua indica, Tectona grandis, Terminalia belerica, Pterocarpus marsupium, Buchanania lanzan, Salmalia malabarica, Emblica officinalis, Mitragyna parviflora, Schleichera oleosa, Miliusa tomentosa, Terminalia arjuna* etc.

2. **Middle canopy** - *Butea monosperma, Zizyphus xylopyra, Elaeodendron glaucoma, Gardenia latifolia, Acacia catechu, Cordia macleodii, Ougeinia oojeinensis, Grewia tiliaefoila, Lagerstroemia parviflora, Bridelia retusa, Aegle marmelos, Cassia fistula, Wrightia tinctoria, Holarrhena antidysentrica, Casearia elliptica* etc.

3. **Shrubs** - *Nyctanthus arbortristis, Lantana camara, Carissa spinarum, Zizyphus marritianna, Woodfordia fruiticosa, Vitex negundo, Grewia hirsuta, Adhatoda vasica* etc.

4. **Bamboo** - *Dendrocalamus strictus* on slopes.

5. **Herbs** - *Cassia tora, Xanthium strumarium, Sida cardifolia* etc.

6. **Grasses** - *Heteropogon contortus, Themeda quadrivalvis, Apluda aristala, Ischacmum rugosum, Sehima nervosum, Cynodon dactylon etc.*

7. **Lianas (woody climbers)** - *Zizyphus oenoplia, Butea superb, Ventilago calyculata, Ichnocarpus frutscens, Celastrus paniculata, Gymnema sylvestris, Smilaz macrophylla, Heruidesnus indicus etc.*

8. **Epiphytes and Parasites -** *Dendrophthoe falcata, Vanda parviflora, Cuscuta reflexa.*

9 781798 005538